I HAVE A CONCUSSION.

NOW WHAT?

JUDY MONROE PETERSON

ROSEN
PUBLISHING®

New York

Published in 2017 by The Rosen Publishing Group, Inc.
29 East 21st Street, New York, NY 10010

Copyright © 2017 by The Rosen Publishing Group, Inc.

First Edition

Library of Congress Cataloging in Publication Data

Names: Peterson, Judy Monroe, author.
Title: I have a concussion, now what? / Judy Monroe Peterson.
Description: First edition. | New York : Rosen Publishing, 2017. | Series: Teen life 411 | Audience: Grades 7–12. | Includes bibliographical references and index.
Identifiers: LCCN 2016023765 | ISBN 9781508171966 (library bound)
Subjects: LCSH: Brain—Concussion—Juvenile literature. | Head—Wounds and injuries—Juvenile literature.
Classification: LCC RC394.C7 P48 2017 | DDC 617.4/81044—dc23
LC record available at https://lccn.loc.gov/2016023765

Manufactured in Malaysia

CONTENTS

Have you ever hit your head hard while playing sports or fallen off a skateboard and then felt dazed or dizzy for a short time? You may have experienced a concussion. Concussions are mild brain injuries usually caused by a bump or blow to the head. They can also occur when the body is jolted or shaken violently, such as in a driving accident. A look inside the head at the time would show the brain rapidly moving back and forth or side-to-side and hitting the hard skull bones. This sudden impact can create chemical changes in the brain and damage brain cells. The result is a concussion, also known as a mild traumatic brain injury (TBI).

Concussions are a large and growing health problem in the United States. The US Centers for Disease Control estimates that 1.6 to 3.8 million people experience sports and recreation-related traumatic brain injury every year, and of those numbers, most are concussions. The numbers are probably much higher, because many people do not get medical care for head injuries. Most teens with a concussion recover quickly and fully. However, sometimes symptoms last months or longer and may lead to short and long-term problems. Athletes who continue to play contact sports, such as boxing or football, may take repeated blows to the head. This could lead to chronic

Some people think athletes can sustain concussions only during team sports. Many concussions also occur during recreational sports. A teen riding a skateboard can fall down and hit his or her head on the ground, resulting in a concussion.

traumatic encephalopathy (CTE), a serious disease that gradually involves more and more nerve cells.

Concussions change brain functions. Teens may experience mild changes, such as feeling dizzy or dazed for a couple of minutes. Other symptoms include ongoing headaches, blurred vision, or irritability. A more severe concussion can lead to memory, speech, problem solving, and balance difficulties. In these cases, people should see a doctor for a medical exam and tests. Depending on the diagnosis, the doctor will help them set up a recovery plan, which usually includes plenty of rest at home. Teens may need to resume school only part-time or limit the amount of schoolwork or homework for some weeks or longer. Restrictions are lifted as they recover. Anyone with serious symptoms, such as convulsions or seizures, should immediately go to a hospital emergency room.

Public awareness of concussions in youth, college, and professional sports, especially in contact sports such as football, hockey, soccer, and boxing, has risen in recent years. Each day, hundreds of thousands of people play, practice, and compete in a large variety of sports. Unfortunately, participation in sporting events raises the risk of getting a concussion. Motor crashes and falls can also result in concussions.

Increasing awareness of concussions and improving the understanding of their effects have resulted in laws in all fifty states that regulate how to recognize and treat these brain injuries. Sports leagues are developing more effective ways to prevent, detect, and treat traumatic brain injuries. During sporting events, everyone—parents, medical staff, coaches, trainers, referees, and players—can prevent concussions by putting safety first. Teens and their families and friends can also get involved to promote greater public knowledge about concussions.

THE NITTY-GRITTY ON CONCUSSIONS

A concussion is a head injury resulting in a temporary loss of brain function. It is a traumatic brain injury (TBI) caused by a bump, blow, or jolt to the head or by a hit to the body that causes the head and brain to move rapidly back and forth inside the skull. The word "concussion" comes from the Latin word *concutere*, which means "to shake violently." Most concussions are mild injuries, but sometimes it can be difficult to determine the extent of the damage at the place of impact. Brain injuries can affect how people think, learn, feel, and act.

UNDERSTANDING THE BRAIN

To understand concussions, it's helpful to know about the brain and how it works. This incredibly complex and powerful organ is the largest part of the nervous system, which is the body's communication network center. The brain receives and processes messages to think, remember, learn, reason, and coordinate muscle movements. It senses changes within and outside the body and can respond in fractions of a second. The brain is necessary for language, solving problems, and creating music and art. All thoughts, moods, emotions, and senses originate in this structure.

An adult brain weighs approximately 3 pounds (1.4 kilograms). It contains about one hundred billion nerve cells, called neurons. These cells transmit and process information between the different parts of the brain.

The brain is similar to both a computer and a chemical plant. The neurons produce electrical signals

The brain constantly receives and analyzes information from the senses about conditions both inside and outside the body. It responds to these messages by allowing people to move, speak, and show emotion.

and send them along pathways called circuits. These circuits receive, process, store, and retrieve information like a computer does. However, the brain creates its electrical signals by chemical means. The proper functioning of the brain depends on the many complicated chemical substances that neurons produce. These tiny substances transmit and process information between parts of the brain. Unlike other cells in the body, neurons cannot replace themselves if damaged.

The human brain looks like a grayish-pink ball with many grooves on its surface. Several protective systems shield it from injuries. Eight hard, rough skull bones protect the soft, jellylike brain, which is also cradled by three layers of membranes called cranial meninges. Cerebrospinal fluid, a colorless liquid between the membranes, cushions the brain from injury. The fluid acts like a shock absorber to keep this structure from hitting the skull when the head moves. The skull bones, cranial meninges, and cerebrospinal fluid work together to protect the brain from everyday bumps. However, these defenses are not enough to fully keep the brain safe from hard hits or jolts.

The Three Parts of the Brain

The cerebrum, cerebellum, and brain stem are the three main areas of the brain. These structures are made up of neurons and other specialized cells that support and protect them.

CEREBRUM

Also called the forebrain, the cerebrum is the largest and most complex part of the brain and sits just below the skull. It controls conscious thought and many kinds of learning. Some regions of the cerebrum are involved in analyzing information, and other parts control fine movements of the body. Different areas help regulate breathing, heart rate, hunger, thirst, and other essential functions.

The cerebrum is divided into two halves called the cerebral hemispheres. A large, thick bundle of nerve fibers connects the hemispheres and allows them to communicate. People use the right hemisphere to interpret information from the senses, such as recognizing faces or appreciating artwork. This region is also concerned with imagination and emotional responses. Teens use their left hemisphere to perform math, logical and critical thinking, abstract reasoning, and language.

The two hemispheres of the cerebrum each contain four lobes: the frontal, temporal, parietal, and occipital. The lobes are named after the bone in the skull that protects them. Because of their nearness to the skull, the frontal and temporal lobes are the ones most often injured in a concussion.

The frontal lobes make it possible to think, learn, concentrate, and reason. The abilities to absorb information in the classroom and solve problems take place here. Teens use the frontal lobes to plan and organize their daily schedules. Emotions are also regulated in this area of the brain, including feeling happy, excited, calm,

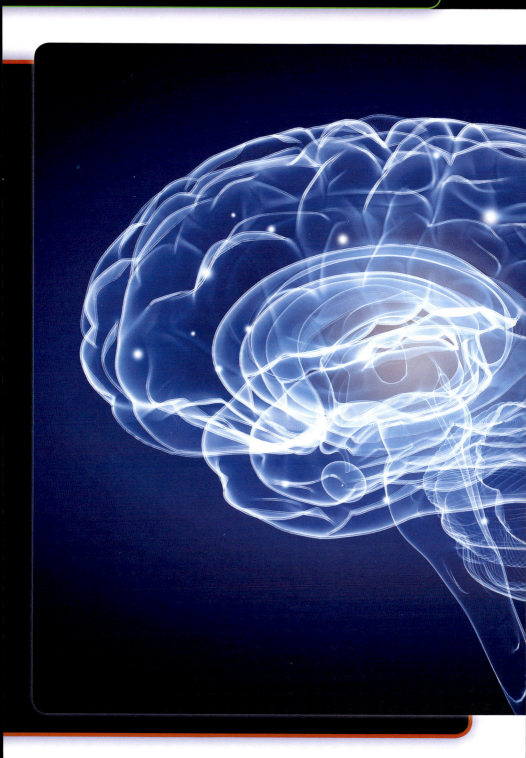

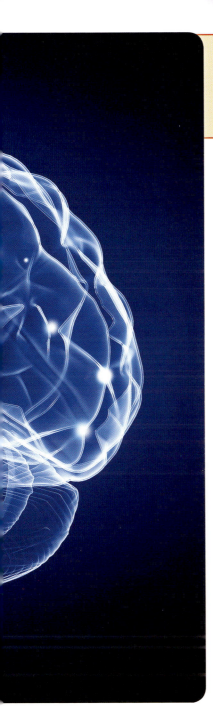

The brain is made up of a number of different regions that all work together to accomplish their tasks. Each area is extremely important and carries out very specific functions.

sad, or angry. The frontal lobes curb inappropriate physical behaviors or impulses. For example, if people suddenly feel furious, they may want to break or hit something. This part of the brain keeps such behaviors under control.

Located near the ears, the temporal lobes are concerned with hearing and how well young people remember events from a long time ago (long-term memory) and what they ate for lunch yesterday (short-term memory). Parietal lobes are involved with a wide variety of sensory information, such as hot, cold, pain, and touch. Injuries here can result in problems with hand-eye coordination and writing. Finally, the occipital lobes sit at the back of the head and deal with vision. When hit in this area, athletes might see stars or flashes of bright light, even though that really does not happen.

Cerebellum

The cerebellum is the second largest region of the brain. This round structure lies at the back of the brain. It is responsible for balance, posture, and the coordination of voluntary muscle movement necessary to walk, talk, jog, run, ski, swim, or kick a football or soccer ball. Like the cerebrum, the cerebellum has a right and a left hemisphere. People with damage to the cerebellum might have uncoordinated, slow

The cerebellum helps maintain the body's sense of balance and coordinates muscular movements with sensory information. It is about the size of an orange and sits slightly above the brain stem.

movements and difficulty with balance. They may need to relearn activities that they easily did before their injury.

Brain Stem

Lying under the cerebellum is the brain stem. It acts as a pathway for messages traveling between other parts of the brain and the spinal cord. The brain stem maintains the heartbeat and blood pressure, digestion, sweating, cyc reflexes, and all other basic functions essential to life. The activities of the brain stem are not under conscious control.

CONCUSSION WARNING SIGNS AND SYMPTOMS

Most concussions are mild injuries and usually not life threatening. Symptoms vary widely and are different for each person. Factors that influence symptoms include the impact of the blow, the part of the brain affected, brain size, body size, gender, and thickness of the skull bones. The symptoms of concussions usually fall into four groups: physical, cognitive and memory, emotional and mood, and sleep.

Physical

A common physical symptom of concussions are headaches, which may continue for weeks or months. Sometimes people say they feel pressure in the head or see flashes of bright lights. Other symptoms include

A hard hit to the head or severe shaking of the body causes the brain to slide violently within its cushioning layers and strike the inside of the hard, bony skull. Brain cells in the outer layer become injured, which affects how they function. Unlike a broken bone in the arm or leg, doctors cannot see concussions on X-rays or imaging scans, because these tests do not show structural damage to the brain.

The brain can slide back and forth, because it sits inside the skull unattached. If a blow or jolt is forceful enough, this organ may be damaged on both the coup side and countercoup side. The coup side is where the impact occurs. When this happens, the brain recoils, lurches backward or forward, and then hits the skull on the opposite side, causing a countercoup. The delicate brain tissue can continue to bounce around and strike the skull in different places. With enough force, it may be injured on both the coup side and the countercoup side.

The jarring of the brain against the sides of the skull can tear blood vessels, pull nerve fibers, and bruise the outside of the brain. This may cause internal bleeding, bruising, or swelling. Severe swelling compresses the brain and its blood vessels. Because the flow of blood is restricted, a stroke can occur. Brain swelling after a serious concussion tends to increase the severity of the injury.

HOW CONCUSSIONS CHANGE THE BRAIN

dizziness, sensitivity to light or noise, or ringing in the ears. Nausea or vomiting can occur, especially early on. Teens may have blurry or fuzzy vision or a fixed stare. Their eyes might look glossy or the pupils become

Symptoms of a concussion vary from subtle to debilitating. This person has a concussion and looks okay. But, he just does not feel right and wants to rest or take a nap.

enlarged or uneven in size. Getting a concussion can make people feel tired or sleepy, move clumsily or too slowly, have poor balance when trying to walk, or briefly lose consciousness. Some young people may slur their speech or have difficulty speaking. In serious cases, repeated vomiting, seizures, or convulsions can occur. Unfortunately, death may even result.

Cognitive and Memory

People use their cognitive abilities to carry out conscious mental activities, such as thinking, reasoning, remembering, imagining, judging, and using language. When a concussion occurs, they may have difficulty concentrating, focusing their attention, or remembering new information. They may ask the same questions repeatedly, but do not understand or remember the answers. Some people experience amnesia and cannot recall what happened before, during, or immediately after experiencing a concussion. Disorientation can also result, which means teens do not know where they are or what is going on. Some athletes say they feel sluggish, foggy, or groggy. Other cognitive symptoms include the inability to solve problems and make decisions. For students, a concussion that affects their cognition may lead to poor academic learning, testing, or performance.

Emotions and Mood

Emotional and behavioral symptoms after a concussion may not occur immediately, but sometimes they are the first signs of brain damage. Teens might have unusual changes in personality and feel nervous or very sad, cry a lot, and are quick to anger. They could become cranky and hard to get along with.

Sleep Problems

People may sleep more or less than usual, have trouble falling asleep, or stay asleep when they have a concussion. A sleep deficit might impact students in many ways, including making it difficult to work on school assignments or take tests. They can have problems concentrating and experience slowed reaction time. Teens could also feel tired and sad.

WHEN TO SEE A DOCTOR

Although the media has heightened awareness of concussions and their associated problems, some people do not yet understand the dangers of these injuries. Teens, parents, coaches, trainers, and school officials need to recognize how serious a concussion can be. Every concussion can injure the brain to some extent. However, most concussions are mild, and people usually recover fully.

Teens participating in sports or other physical activities could sustain minor concussions. However, lingering problems signal that a health care professional should be consulted.

Everyone who participates in contact and recreational sports, such as bicycling, skiing, or skateboarding, should know the common signs and symptoms of concussion. These include nausea, vomiting, dizziness, confusion, headache, slowed thinking, memory loss, sensitivity to light or noise, and sleeping difficulties. Teens can become irritable or depressed or have mood swings. If any of these symptoms appear after a blow or jolt to the head or body, people should see a health care professional. Symptoms can also worsen over hours or days.

It's important for anyone with possible brain damage to be evaluated by a medical professional, even if emergency care is not required. A doctor can rule out a more serious brain injury, many of which have similar initial symptoms.

Some symptoms that may indicate a severe brain injury has occurred include feeling extremely sleepy, sick, weak, numb, confused, or restless. Other danger signs are one pupil larger than the other, a severe headache that will not go away, slurred speech, or clumsiness. Young people might have repeated vomiting, convulsions, seizures, and sometimes loss of consciousness. If any of these symptoms appear, a coach, trainer, parent, or other adult must get immediate medical attention by calling 911 for emergency medical services or taking them directly to the local hospital emergency room.

MYTHS AND FACTS

MYTH

Everyone loses consciousness during a concussion.

FACT

Only about 10 percent of those people who experience a concussion lose consciousness or black out. Years ago, it was commonly believed that being knocked unconscious was the only sign of a concussion.

MYTH

People can rely on smartphone apps to diagnose and treat a concussion.

FACT

Smartphone apps, such as the ImPACT concussion tool, can be used to document the immediate symptoms of a possible concussion. A medical professional can use this information to diagnosis and treat a concussion.

MYTH

Athletes show strength and courage when they get a hard blow or jolt and continue to play.

FACT

Playing while in pain puts athletes at risk for a concussion and other serious injuries.

CHAPTER 2

CAUSES: SPORTS AND BEYOND

Concussions are a large problem in the United States. They can happen to anyone at any age and often with no advance warning. Concussions most often occur from incidents associated with motor vehicle accidents, falls, and many types of sports. Sometimes people sustain concussions because of earthquakes, tornadoes, floods, and other forces out of their control. Carelessness like running on an icy sidewalk, or the serious potential for danger, such as driving while drinking or texting, can result in a hard blow or jolt to the head or body.

A PREVALENT ISSUE

According to the Centers for Disease Control and Prevention, about 2.2 million Americans go to emergency departments each year for traumatic brain injuries. Of that number, more than five hundred thousand youth between the ages of eight and nineteen visit emergency rooms for concussions. The agency estimates the rate of concussions in children has risen nearly 60 percent since the early 2000s. Health care professionals think these sobering statistics mean that concussions are a worrisome epidemic. Student athletes are much more susceptible to head injuries than professionals because their bodies and nervous systems, including the brain, are still developing. Undiagnosed concussions can affect the performance of young people in school and on and off the athletic field.

When natural disasters strike, flying debris can cause many people to sustain head injuries. Heavy flooding from a monsoon rain in Thailand resulted in many injuries and deaths.

A variety of factors are likely contributing to the rising incidence of concussion. The higher rates may be because parents, health care professionals, trainers, and coaches have a better understanding and more accurately report concussions. Also, concussions are a media concern today, because more attention is being given to the topic from the federal government, National Football League, National Federation of State High School Associations, and other organizations.

However, current concussion statistics are probably too low. One factor feeding into the incorrect incidence rates is that people go to various health care facilities, such as emergency rooms, trauma centers, urgent care clinics, and doctors' offices. Medical staff in different settings may miss diagnosing concussions. Unlike a broken ankle, concussions are not visible by standard imaging tools. Also, consistent medical definition of concussion does not exist. Several national organizations have published definitions, but some doctors do not regularly use them.

Risk-Taking Behaviors

Most concussions in young people occur from falls, motor vehicle accidents, and sports. Teens tend to experience concussions at a greater rate than adults, which could be related to their risk-taking behaviors. As children develop into teens, they tend to move from lower to higher chances of having concussions. Little kids might safely pedal a tricycle, but as older teens, some ride motorcycles, which presents a greater chance of resulting in a serious motor accident. Older teens and young adults have more opportunities to engage in risky behaviors because they have less supervision by their parents than children and younger teens do.

For teens, adolescence is a time of experimentation and change. Age, level of maturity, emotions, personality, and past experiences all feed into the process of making decisions about the actions they take. Their behaviors and the consequences can help them learn how to interact with peers and other people and understand more about themselves. Young people may enter uncertain situations to discover whether they might gain something. This desire for rewards and tolerance for the unknown can help them mature, but it also increases their chance of danger. For example, a young girl might play in an unsupervised game of tackle football to test her abilities, although she likely weighs less and is much shorter than the other male players.

Teens also need and want emotional independence from parents, although they still want their support. During adolescence, they learn to form more mature relationships with different people, including their peers. Peer pressure is a powerful force. Most young people want to fit in, be accepted, and have the approval of others. Friendship often takes on great importance during the teen years, which is also the time when they search for identities and a sense of belonging. Having friends is essential.

As young people mature, their physical activities become a little rougher. These factors, combined with risk-taking behaviors, may result in head injuries.

When some teens think about taking risky behaviors, they may be influenced by what their peers are saying or doing. Peer pressure can be a powerful motivator. This could lead youth to behave in a way they know isn't right or safe, but gains them approval or acceptance from their peers. Participating in high-risk situations can result because teens do not have enough information to make informed choices. Or, they can feel emotional over an issue, which sometimes clouds their judgement and leads to making unsound decisions. Some young people overestimate their ability to identify and avoid a potentially dangerous situation. They may believe they are invincible or nothing bad will happen to them. They do not think about the possible negative consequences of their choices.

TEENS AND SPORTS

Many teens enjoy being physically active. All types of sports provide exercise and benefit the body and mind. Being physically fit helps young people stay healthy, learn discipline, set and achieve goals, and do well in school. Since many sports involve working or playing with other people, they can be a positive way to socialize. Involvement in sports also provides people with useful skills to be successful in school, on the job, and throughout their lives.

Teens can choose from a multitude of sports. Some join teams to play contact sports, such as football,

Sports usually involve competition and are guided by a set of rules. Whatever sport people choose to play, the physical activity can help keep their minds and bodies fit. And participating in sports is fun!

hockey, soccer, basketball, lacrosse, rugby, or wrestling. Nature sports are popular, including skating, skiing, sailing, surfing, rock climbing, rollerblading, skateboarding, and snowboarding. Tennis and racquetball are partner sports, because they are carried out with another person. People can participate in bicycling, playing golf, jogging, swimming, or other individualized sports. Many young people enjoy more than one type of sport. That's good! Alternating physical activities works different muscles and body systems and helps keep physical activity routines from becoming boring, which helps reduce the likelihood of injury from focusing on only one sport.

However, getting a concussion is a risk in almost every sport, from youth to professional sports. The American Association of Neurological Surgeons estimates that the chance of a concussion for someone playing in a contact sport could be as high as 19 percent per year of play. More than sixty-two thousand concussions occur every year in high school sports.

Contact Sports and Concussions

Media coverage and public awareness of concussions in contact sports has been increasing in recent years. One sport under scrutiny is professional football. In this intense and fast-moving game, large, strong players hit or collide with each other using great force. Studies by the National Football League show that a striking player in open-field collisions can travel an average of about twenty miles (thirty-two kilometers) per hour. The head of the opposing player absorbs most of the blow's energy, which can lead to a concussion. The quality and nature of playing surfaces also has a powerful impact upon concussion rates and prevalence.

Concussions in football are not limited to the pros. Football is the number one participation sport in the nation's high schools. The National Federation of State High School Associations reports that more than one million high school athletes play football during the season. And, football has the highest rate of sports-related concussions compared to any other sports.

According to different studies, concussion rates vary considerably by the type of contact sport and gender of the high school athletes. However, researchers have found similar results. After football, males playing ice hockey, lacrosse, wrestling, soccer, and rugby have the highest incidences of concussions. Rates are lower in basketball and baseball. For females, the highest rate of concussions occurs in soccer, followed by lacrosse and basketball. A major reason for high concussion rates in soccer is heading, practiced by both males and females. To direct a moving ball, players contact it on the forehead at or near the hairline.

Girls have a higher rate of concussion than boys in soccer and basketball. The reason for this is not clear. Some scientists think it is because females tend to have weaker neck muscles to support their head than males. The neck muscles absorb some of the energy from a blow or jolt, which helps keep the brain from sliding around. Other experts believe that girls are simply more honest about reporting their injuries than boys are. Yet another factor is that concussion symptoms of females seem to be worse and last longer than those of males. This could mean that girl players have more time to report their symptoms to coaches and trainers than boys.

OTHER RISK FACTORS

The major risk factors for experiencing a concussion are different depending on the age group. In babies, the main cause of concussion is shaken baby syndrome, in which they are shaken violently and repeatedly, followed by falls and motor vehicle accidents. The chief causes of concussions in older children are physical abuse, traffic accidents, and falls. By the age of ten, many children are involved in one or more sports played on a field, court, or rink. Individual sports also become more popular, such as skating, skiing, gymnastics, karate, dance, skateboarding, or horseback riding. Playing two or more sports increases the risk of concussion because the chance of having a hard hit to the head rises.

Motor vehicle accidents are the leading cause of concussions in teens and young adults, which often result from not wearing seatbelts, inattention while texting or talking, or driving under the influence of alcohol or drugs. Impaired thinking and judgment from drinking alcohol and drug use leads to an increase in accidents and injuries. Falls are another way young people sustain a concussion. They might fall while playing sports or

The number of concussions in sports is probably much higher than what is currently reported. In the past, many players, coaches, parents, and other people did not think concussions were serious. Most people did not know much about them, and the word "concussion" was seldom used. Youth, high school, and professional athletes were encouraged to be tough and continue to play, even if they felt dizzy or ill after getting hit in the head or slammed to the ground. If pulled from a game, they often were allowed to return after only several minutes of sitting on the bench if they seemed symptom free. The emphasis in sports was on shaking it off, meaning to ignore injures and get back into the game. This unwritten code among players was the norm in boxing, football, ice hockey, and other contact sports. Slang terms used to describe a concussion reflected a lack of understanding about the possible seriousness of brain injuries. Examples of these terms include getting his "bell rung" or that she was "dinged" or had a "dinger." Although much more information about concussions is available today, sometimes athletes of all ages try to hide their symptoms or fail to report them to avoid sitting out a play or even a whole game, losing their spot in a lineup, or looking weak. They know other teammates get hit hard in the head and play through their pain. Also, s might feel they are letting their teammates down by not participating in practices or games as they did before. At the start of each season, coaches and trainers should discuss the signs and symptoms of concussions with their athletes. They need to encourage everyone to stop playing immediately and inform sports staff if they or someone else has possible concussion symptoms.

KEEPING BRAIN INJURIES SECRET IN SPORTS

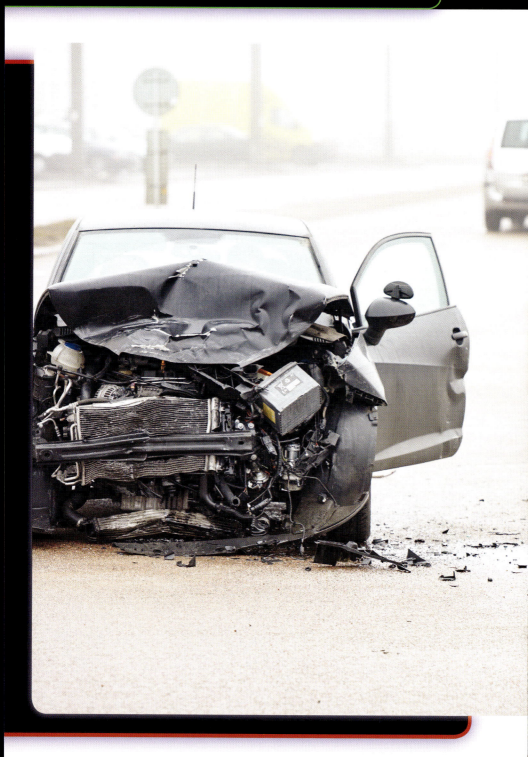

Traffic accidents are a major cause of brain injuries across all age groups. A teen might cause a collision because he or she is learning how to drive, which takes skill and experience.

while biking, skateboarding, snowboarding, or surfboarding. Playing football, boxing, wrestling, ice hockey, lacrosse, rugby and other fast-moving contact sports greatly increases the risk of brain injury. Players could get knocked down, tackled, or hit hard with sports equipment, such as a lacrosse stick or puck, and sustain concussions.

CHAPTER 3

TESTING AND DIAGNOSIS

Getting a correct diagnosis by a medical professional is critical for determining how best to manage a concussion. The sooner someone is evaluated, the quicker treatment can begin. In turn, this can help lessen the effects of the injury.

Coaches, athletic trainers, and parents should know the symptoms of concussions and get medical help for a young athlete when needed. It is critical to call 911 or go to the emergency room right away if the injured teen has a severe headache, confusion, or other concussion symptoms that are getting worse over time. Symptoms that require immediate medical care include repeated vomiting, seizures, or if the pupils of the eyes are different sizes.

If you think you have a concussion, promptly stop what you are doing and tell your trainer, coach, school nurse, teacher, parent, guardian, or another adult. Then get a medical checkup as soon as possible.

SIDELINE TESTING IN SPORTS

Many concussions young people experience occur while playing team sports. It's important for athletic trainers or coaches to quickly assess athletes for a concussion, particularly in collisions, wherever the injury happened. The use of sideline testing is common in school and sports leagues. By observing players and doing a few

Athletic trainers are often the first line of defense to determine if an athlete has sustained a brain injury. They are trained in the identification of concussions.

When an athlete at a sporting event receives a hard blow to the head, athletic trainers and coaches can provide an immediate evaluation to decide if a player needs medical help.

simple tests, trained staff can quickly determine if medical care is needed. The wrong decision could mean extra weeks or months of recovery for athletes. Staff should always follow the rule, "When in doubt, sit them out," because the safety of athletes is always more important than winning a game.

During sideline testing, trainers or coaches might see if players can walk in a straight line or count to ten. They often ask questions to test time and place orientation. Some of the questions include: "What color is the jersey of the opposing team?" "What is the score?" "Who scored most recently?" "What month is it?" "What is the date today?" "Did your team win the last game?" Athletes with symptoms of a concussion are immediately pulled from the game and asked to see a doctor. They cannot return to play until cleared by a medical professional.

BASELINE TESTING

Baseline testing is a helpful tool in the management of concussions. These exams measure an athlete's balance, learning and memory skills, ability to pay attention and concentrate, and the time it takes to solve problems. They also test for concussion symptoms. Trained health care professionals supervise the tests, which are best conducted preseason before the first practice. The results provide a baseline (starting point) to compare similar test results during the season if an athlete has a suspected concussion. After evaluating the information, health care professionals can determine the degree of brain injury.

Baseline testing is common at the professional and college level, and it is being used by a growing number of high schools. Different computerized baseline tests are available. Examples include Post-Concussion Assessment and Cognitive Testing (ImPACT), SCORE, Computerized Cognitive Assessment Tool (CCAT), and Concussion Resolution Index (CRI). These exams are of special importance for teens competing in contact and collision sports, especially football, ice hockey, soccer, lacrosse, wrestling, and basketball.

There are no correct or incorrect answers in baseline testing. However, sometimes players purposely do not do well on the tests. That way, the difference between

Athletic trainers are injury specialists, and they work in every sport. Their job is to pay attention to every play of a game, which allows them to see injuries as they occur. They are responsible for pulling athletes out of a game and requesting a concussion evaluation by a doctor. Sometimes athletes want to continue playing, or coaches pressure them to return to the game, but trainers make those decisions based on what they think is best for the players. Each professional sports team has at least two athletic trainers per team, and colleges have specific trainers assigned to each sport. Many larger high school teams have trainers. In some states, trainers working in high schools are not expected to attend multiple games. Instead, they are sent to the sporting events that have the highest likelihood of injuries. Football is the first priority. Next is hockey before basketball and soccer followed by baseball.

Athletic trainers study specific injuries in different sports and work with doctors on how to prevent, assess, and treat them. Most states regulate the profession of athletic training. Trainers must earn a degree from a college or university within a qualified athletic training program. Many also earn a master's degree. To remain certified, they are required to work under the direction of a physician within their state laws and take ongoing education refresher courses.

ATHLETIC TRAINERS

the two exams is not as stark, and they will be allowed to keep playing after a hard hit to the head. It's extremely important that the no-pain, no-gain, stoic culture of young athletes is changed. Self-reporting and self-protection need to be encouraged and respected over doing and saying anything to stay in the game. Teammates should not think of someone who reports a possible concussion as weak, a quitter, or a whiner. Such value shifts need to come from coaches, parents, and players. Sometimes athletes think they are not fully recovered from a concussion, but feel pressured by their coach to resume playing. Everyone has the right to refuse playing without the fear of retribution and should be provided time to talk with a doctor, if necessary.

Health professionals are testing goggles that can detect a concussion immediately at the site of injury and determine whether an athlete can continue to play.

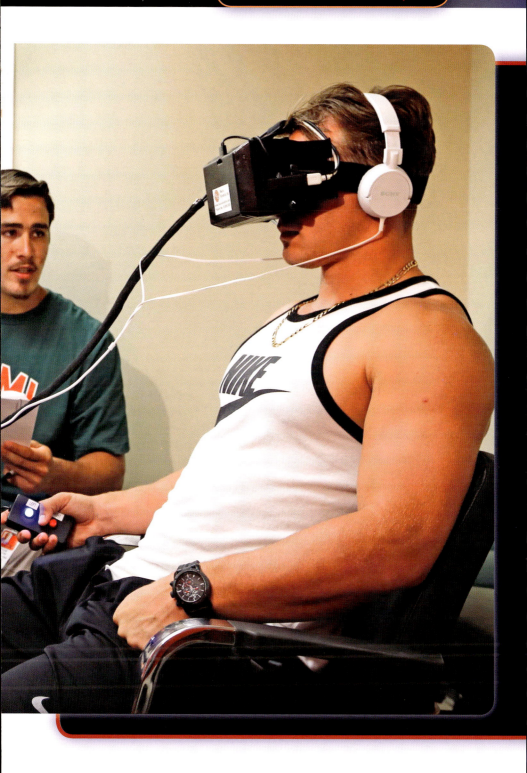

Before an Appointment

The first health care professional that people see for a concussion assessment is usually a doctor. It's essential to rest as much as possible while waiting for the appointment. Everyone should avoid playing any sports, taking long walks, weightlifting, or doing other physical activities that increase the heart rate. Light, simple meals and sleeping in a quiet, dark room are useful during this time.

Athletes should also reduce any activities that can make their symptoms worse, especially if focused attention is required. This includes computer work, schoolwork, watching TV or movies, playing video games, texting, or driving. Taking acetaminophen is the best medication for reducing headache pain.

To prepare for an appointment, teens or their parents or guardians can write down important information about the signs and symptoms of the possible concussion. They should record when the symptoms began and how long they lasted. Problems with lights or sound, memory, concentration, sleeping, or mood changes are critical to tell the doctor. Bringing other key information along is extremely helpful, including previous head injuries, the current treatment for ongoing medical conditions, and the names of any current medications, vitamins, or supplements.

Sometimes teens set up an appointment for a concussion assessment, but their symptoms increase or new ones appear before then. For example, they might have a worsening headache, numbness, or weakness. Staying safe is their top priority. Young people need not wait for the future appointment, but should ask a parent or another adult for help, call 911, or get to their local hospital emergency room immediately.

WHAT HAPPENS DURING AN APPOINTMENT

Getting a correct diagnosis for a concussion is critical. Doctors can then recommend the best treatment and minimize further damage to the brain. During the appointment, the medical professionals ask about symptoms, when they started, their severity, and if they are becoming worse. They also want to know about a teen's general physical and mental health, medical history, family history, prescription medications, and alcohol or illegal drug use. Doctors also conduct a physical exam and laboratory tests to rule out other conditions, such as dehydration or lack of sleep.

Next, health care professionals may perform or recommend a series of tests. Neurologists conduct exams to uncover problems with vision, hearing, reflexes, balance, strength, and coordination. Several neuropsychological exams may be given to evaluate a variety of cognitive (thinking) abilities, including speed of information processing, attention, memory, recall, and language. Teens and their parents should feel free to ask the doctor questions at any time.

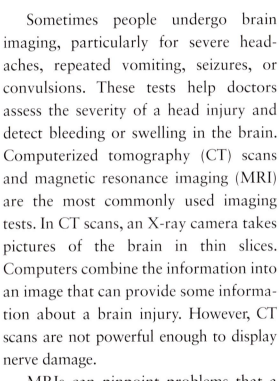

An athlete might undergo a computerized tomography (CT) scan when hit hard on the head. He or she would lie on a movable table that allows accurate positioning of the head within the machine.

Sometimes people undergo brain imaging, particularly for severe headaches, repeated vomiting, seizures, or convulsions. These tests help doctors assess the severity of a head injury and detect bleeding or swelling in the brain. Computerized tomography (CT) scans and magnetic resonance imaging (MRI) are the most commonly used imaging tests. In CT scans, an X-ray camera takes pictures of the brain in thin slices. Computers combine the information into an image that can provide some information about a brain injury. However, CT scans are not powerful enough to display nerve damage.

MRIs can pinpoint problems that a CT scan cannot detect. MRIs use powerful magnets and radio waves to chart the energy in the brain, which is used to produce computerized, detailed pictures of the brain. This information helps doctors find bleeding or swelling. However, CT scans and MRIs may not show cognitive damage caused by brain injuries.

Making a Diagnosis

Determining whether teens have a concussion can be complicated. Unless some scrapes or bruises appear on the head or face after a fall or blow to the head, mild brain injuries are often invisible. Concussions vary in their location, type, and extent of damage. Everyone develops a unique mix of symptoms. Physicians make a diagnosis based on the symptoms, medical history, and results from a physical exam and various tests.

When patients who sustained concussions are discharged from the hospital, physicians provide them with information about what to expect after the concussion.

Making a diagnosis can sometimes be tricky. Symptoms may not appear until hours or days after a hard blow or jolt occurred. Another issue is the lack of specific laboratory tests that prove a concussion happened. To date, medical professionals do not have a foolproof way to diagnose these brain injuries.

After a Diagnosis

Some people with a concussion need to be hospitalized overnight for observation. If the doctor agrees that the teens can be watched at home, someone should stay with them for at least twenty-four hours and make sure symptoms are not becoming worse. The physician can provide information on what the caregiver should do during this critical time.

After a diagnosis, the concussed teens and everyone around them should know the concussion symptoms that can escalate and require a trip to the emergency room. It's also critical to know that the mental state of concussed athletes may change hours or days after the concussion occurred. They might not view the situation as urgent, but it still may be very serious.

CHAPTER 4

CONSEQUENCES

Many people have a concussion and never even know about it because their symptoms disappear within a few hours. Most concussions, including those that occur during youth sports, are usually mild and disappear within several weeks. Teens may miss one or two practices or even a game during this time, but then easily resume their regular activities. However, even a mild head injury can cause serious problems. If the brain swells, blood vessels in the brain can tear and blood leaks into the skull cavity, leading to dangerous situations. Some people develop lingering or extremely severe symptoms, which can become permanent. Research is ongoing to better understand the short-term and long-term effects of concussions.

POSTCONCUSSION SYNDROME (PCS)

Within days to weeks after a concussion occurs, teens can develop a variety of symptoms called postconcussion syndrome. Most teens fully recover within several weeks and return to their usual activities, including sports. Other people

When a concussion has been diagnosed, teens are strongly advised to avoid physical and mental work. Instead, they should rest and sleep, which allows the brain time to heal itself.

take longer to heal, and their complications could continue for months. The majority of symptoms seldom linger beyond a year. Researchers have found that young people who do not take enough time to rest and heal their brain after a concussion increase their chance of developing this complex disorder.

Postconcussion syndrome can cause a wide variety of physical, cognitive, and emotional problems that affect daily life. For example, some teens do not function as well as they did before getting a head injury. They may have difficulty performing well at school or work, or in sports. Or relationships with friends and family can become negative.

Concussed teens might be bothered by one or more

persistent symptoms or new ones may appear. The most common symptom is headache. They may also feel dizzy, extremely tired, and confused, or have some memory loss or difficulties concentrating, paying attention, or coping with stress. They may have blurry vision, sensitivity to light or sound, or irregular sleep patterns. Friends and family may notice personality changes for no clear reason, such as irritability, restlessness, anxiety, or depression.

Even the best athletes can experience persistent symptoms caused by post-concussion syndrome. According to an article by Pat Borzi in the *New York Times*, Amanda Kessel was rated college hockey's top female player in 2013. She had played ice hockey for the Minnesota Golden Gophers in the 2013 National College Athletic Association. The following year, she experienced a concussion during the 2014 Sochi Olympics. Her team won the gold medal game, but continued post-concussion symptoms kept Amanda off the ice for a year.

LINGERING COGNITIVE AND PHYSICAL EFFECTS

Most teens with negative effects caused by a concussion fully recovery. It is important to know that only a minority of people develop severe postconcussion symptoms, and of this group, fewer have permanent problems. In the vast majority of cases, concussion issues disappear over time.

Common cognitive and physical symptoms that sometimes linger after a concussion include headache and feeling tired and less alert. When a concussion occurs, brain functions can become damaged, and the thinking processes and memory pathways in the brain slow down. This can cause some students to take a longer time to process information. They may have difficulty with problem solving, concentrating, learning, and recalling what they have learned, and they can easily become confused

A young person who has difficulty concentrating on his or her classroom studies after receiving a hard hit to the head might have a concussion.

or distracted. Teens might make more errors with their schoolwork and on tests. As a result, their grades could drop. When some young people with postconcussion syndrome try to keep up in school, they become stressed and their symptoms become worse.

Other lingering complications can follow a concussion, such as dizziness, sensitivity to light or noise, or problems with balance. Issues may occur with spoken or written words. Young people might slur their words, speak too slowly, or have difficulty understanding, remembering, or speaking. Teens might also react slower than before a concussion, and their problem-solving and decision-making abilities become impaired. They could take greater risks because their judgment is affected and that increases their chance of causing or being in a motor vehicle accident.

MOOD AND BEHAVIOR PROBLEMS

Even mild concussions can leave people with emotional and behavioral symptoms for weeks, months, or longer. Mood swings and unpleasant personality changes could occur, such as irrational behavior, crying jags, or unusual flashes of anger or bouts of shouting. Young people could act out or feel overly irritable, grumpy, or anxious. They can become easily impatient, frustrated, or distracted.

Sometimes young people feel depressed and become irrational and withdraw from friends, family, and school activities. They may fall into reckless behavior. The depression could be caused by having sustained a concussion.

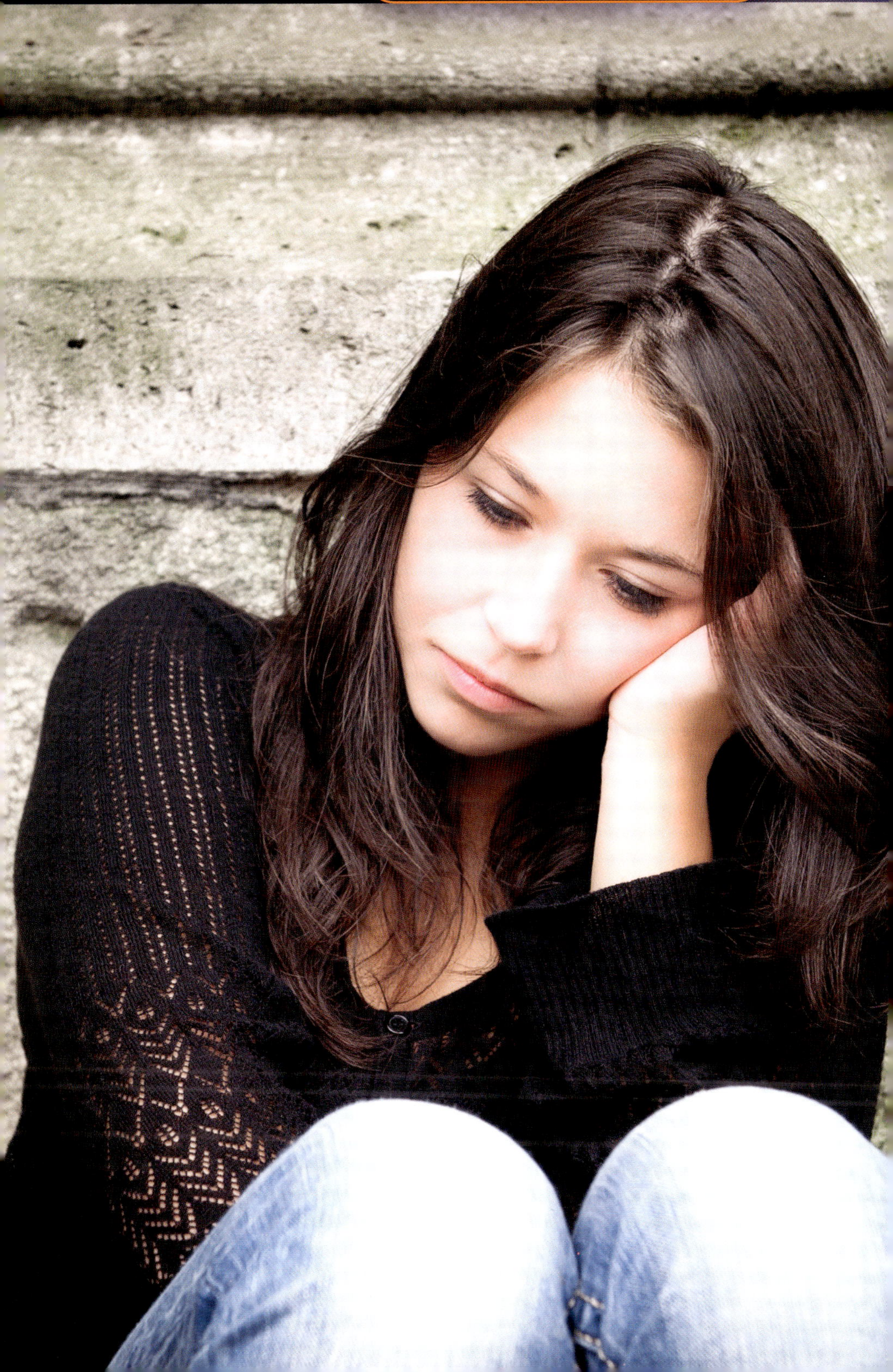

Signs of depression after a concussion are common. Everyone occasionally feels sad, unhappy, stressed, or overwhelmed with the challenges and responsibilities of everyday life. Most people can successfully cope with their ups and downs and do not remain sad for long periods of time. Teens are considered depressed when their symptoms last more than two weeks and interfere with their daily life.

Some young people who are depressed feel sad, very tired, worthless, or overly anxious most of the time. They may lose interest in activities and hobbies that once were fun and sleep or eat too little or too much. Other symptoms include irritability, anger, and difficulty concentrating or making decisions. Depression negatively affects behaviors at school, at home, and in social relationships. These issues might cause the teens to experience increased problems with peer and adult relationships and handling social situations.

Sometimes concussed teens feel exceedingly isolated and hopeless. They spend less and less time with friends and withdraw from their family. People can fall into deep despair or hopelessness if their negative feelings spiral downward and continue for long periods of time. Their depression is now considered a medical illness. If left untreated, their risk increases for suicidal thoughts, behaviors, and even committing suicide. For example, in 2015, retired National Football League quarterback Erik Kramer, at age fifty, attempted suicide, but survived. He had played ten seasons during his football career. After leaving football, he battled depression for years that stemmed from repeated brain injuries he had as a pro football player.

CHRONIC TRAUMATIC ENCEPHALOPATHY (CTE)

Chronic traumatic encephalopathy (CTE) is a progressive, degenerative disease of the brain. It destroys more and more brain cells and cannot be stopped or reversed. Brain functions decline, leading to increased problems with thinking, movement, emotions, and speaking. CTE is caused by repeated blows to the head for many years. As head traumas continue over time, a protein in the brain called tau builds up and interferes with brain functioning. There is no cure for this disease. It is important for you to know that the majority of people with a history of recurring concussions are unlikely to develop CTE.

Once called punch drunk syndrome, chronic traumatic encephalopathy was first detected in boxers during the 1920s. Doctors now know that active and retired pro athletes in a variety of sports that involve repeated hits to the head, such as boxing and football, have an increased risk of developing the disease. The incidence of CTE is unknown, because a diagnosis can only be made by examining a brain after death. Researchers are working on ways to diagnose the disease in people who are still alive.

Symptoms of CTE usually are not evident right away. But, over time, difficulties with thinking, memory, behaviors, and emotions begin and worsen. Intense headaches

SECOND IMPACT SYNDROME

Second impact syndrome is the dangerous result of having a second concussion before the brain has healed from a first concussion. This condition is extremely rare, but can lead to permanent brain damage, convulsions, coma, or even death. It is caused by severe brain swelling that restricts the circulation of blood within the brain. Second impact syndrome is life-threatening and requires surgery to prevent further injury to the brain. Even if the second hit to the brain is mild, symptoms can develop rapidly and may be difficult to control. Sometimes second impact syndrome appears days to weeks after a first concussion is diagnosed. Common symptoms of this condition include loss of eye movement, dilated pupils, or severe breathing difficulties. People can become unconscious and even die.

The risk of post-secondary syndrome is higher in some sports, such as boxing, football, hockey, soccer, skiing, baseball or snowboarding. This syndrome occurs mainly in children and teens. Experts are not sure why this happens. One reason could be that many mild concussions are not diagnosed in these age groups, and the brain does not have adequate recovery time before the next concussion occurs. Also, concussions usually take longer to heal in young people than adults, because their brains are still growing and developing. This may increase the chance of incomplete healing before experiencing another concussion.

and moodiness occur, including crying, irritability, and anger. People develop dementia, become confused, behave impulsively, or have violent outbursts. Speech and coordination are affected. Severe depression is another complication of CTE, which can lead to the abuse or addiction of alcohol or drugs or dangerous suicidal thoughts or actions. Sadly, some deeply depressed athletes have taken their own lives.

LEARNING MORE ABOUT CHRONIC TRAUMATIC ENCEPHALOPATHY

Chronic traumatic encephalopathy was discovered by Dr. Bennet Omalu, a neurologist. These medical doctors are experts on diseases of the brain and nervous system. In 2002, the physician was examining the brain of pro football player Mike Webster to establish the cause of death. The athlete had played seventeen years for the National Football League and was in the Pro Football Hall of Fame. After retiring, the former football star began to behave in troubling ways. As his cognitive abilities deteriorated, he became severely depressed. Dr. Omalu determined that the athlete had chronic traumatic encephalopathy. The physician soon found the same disease in another pro football player. Since then, the brains of other deceased football greats have been diagnosed with CTE, including Junior Seau, Frank Gifford, Ken Stabler, and Ray Easterling.

At first, the NFL denied a link between repeated concussions and CTE. However, in a 2015 lawsuit, the league agreed to pay up to $5 million per retired player for severe medical conditions associated with repeated head injury. This announcement caused some active football players to rethink their career choice and take action. For example, in that same year, Chris Borland, a talented rookie pro NFL player, resigned after only one season of play. He wanted to avoid getting repeated head blows that can cause permanent brain injuries linked to CTE. In 2016, the NFL finally agreed that a connection exists between football-related trauma and brain disease that leads to CTE. In that same year, standout Husain Abdullah, age thirty-two, announced his retirement because of worries about the numerous concussions he sustained.

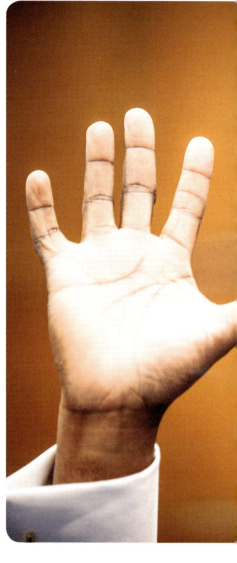

Chronic traumatic encephalopathy is not limited to pro football. Athletes from other sports have had the same diagnosis, including former National Hockey League player Steve Montador, Major League Baseball player Ryan Freel, and wrestler Chris Benoit. The disease has also been discovered in the brains of deceased college and high school football players.

People have known about brain damage caused by concussions since the 1920s. About eighty years later, Bennet Omalu provided the first physical evidence of chronic traumatic encephalopathy, a devastating brain disease, in pro football players.

Several institutions are studying CTE and working to find ways to prevent it. Boston University established a CTE program which shares a brain bank with the Concussion Legacy Foundation and the Department of Veterans Affairs. An increasing number of active and retired pro athletes have donated or announced their intention to donate their brain, after death, to the shared brain bank. In 2016, retired women's soccer stars Cindy Parlow and Brandi Chastain pledged to donate their brains to help researchers understand the effects of repeated injuries to brain tissue and the development of CTE. To date, few female brains have been donated and researchers lack information on how gender affects the development of CTE.

10 GREAT QUESTIONS TO ASK A PHYSICIAN

1. What treatments are available for my concussion and which do you recommend?

2. Do you have any good resources on concussions that you can recommend?

3. What lifestyle changes should I make to manage my concussion?

4. What is the risk of future concussions?

5. Is my condition temporary or chronic? How will it progress over time?

6. Do I have to give up playing my favorite sport?

7. What medical treatments are available for my concussion and which do you recommend?

8. What should I do if concussion symptoms return?

9. What kind of neurological tests will you perform?

10. What kinds of medicine are safe for me to take?

CHAPTER 5

HEALING THE BRAIN

Chemicals in the brain change after a concussion occurs. This causes the brain's usual functions to become disorganized, and it experiences problems performing as it used to. Concussed people may have difficulty absorbing information, making sense of it, and following through with appropriate behavior. During recovery, symptoms in student athletes can continue for several weeks or longer. It's important not to rush the healing process.

IMMEDIATELY AFTER A CONCUSSION OCCURS

Teens require complete rest and lots of sleep for a minimum of twenty-four hours immediately after a concussion. They should avoid playing sports, working out, or doing chores around the home. Cognitive rest is also key. This means staying clear of work, schoolwork, TV, movies, video games, texting, or reading.

To help reduce headache pain, physicians may suggest prescription medicine or a nonprescription pain reliever, such as acetaminophen. Injured players need to avoid aspirin, ibuprofen, or other over-the-counter pain relievers, because these medications could increase the chance of bleeding in the brain if a head injury has occurred. Ice or cold packs placed on the head or neck for ten to twenty minutes at a time can help ease headache pain.

When a concussion has occurred, it is critical that injured teens carefully follow their doctor's treatment plans, including using the correct prescription and nonprescription medications.

Recovery

Doctors work with young people to set up a concussion recovery plan. Just like people should rest a sprained wrist, the best way to heal the brain after a concussion is rest. Avoiding activities that might cause additional head injury is important, because the brain is more sensitive to damage during the healing process. The good news is that the vast majority of people with a concussion recover without any lasting effects.

Many injured players want to know when they can play their favorite sports again. It's usually difficult for health care professionals to determine exactly how long it will take to recover from a concussion, because the rate of recovery differs for each person. There is no clear timeline for a safe return to normal activities. Medical professionals evaluate the healing process on a case-by-case basis. Severely hurt or destroyed brain tissue seldom regenerates, meaning new brain cells cannot form. Sometimes, especially in young people, other areas of the brain might make up for the injured tissue. The brain may learn to reroute information in new ways and bypass the damaged areas.

Repair of the brain depends on many factors, including the location and severity of the injury, concussion history, sports played, treatment, whether symptoms return during the recovery process, and how quickly symptoms disappear. Memory loss caused by a concussion can be distressing, but it is usually temporary. Because the brain continues to develop in young people, medical professionals usually need to treat their concussions longer than those in adults.

RETURN TO PLAY AND ACTIVITY GUIDELINES

Experts agree that athletes must not return to their regular activity and sports until symptoms are totally gone at rest and during exercise. Physicians and athletic trainers often use a five-step recovery plan based on the US Centers for Disease Control (CDC) program called HEADS UP. This program provides a set of Return to Play Progression guidelines for concussed athletes. The steps can be individualized to fit various situations. The athletic department in your school likely has an established return-to-play procedure based on the CDC plan.

The goal of HEADS UP is to slowly and safely get players back to their regular activities, including playing sports. Each of the five steps requires a minimum of twenty-four hours to complete. Teens can move to the next level after they remain free of symptoms at their current step. If any symptoms reappear, they need to stop and return to the previous level.

Before the plan begins, a baseline must be established. This requires players to have complete rest without any stressful mental or physical activity until all symptoms of their concussion disappear. After a concussion, students may need to stay home from school and avoid any social functions for a minimum of

twenty-four hours. A symptom-free starting point is extremely important, because getting too little rest can extend the recovery process. Once a baseline is established, young people can begin the Return to Play plan. It can take several weeks or longer to work through the entire process. Here are the five steps of the process:

1. Everyone can start with light exercise for five to ten minutes. Suggested activities include easy, slow walking, light jogging, and stationary biking. They should avoid lifting weights, running, or jumping.
2. Moderate exercise comes next. Performing activities that slightly increase the heart rate are OK, such as moderate jogging, weight lifting, or exercise bicycling.
3. More intense exercise is allowed, including running, regular weight lifting, intense stationary biking, and noncontact practice drills.
4. Athletes can participate in full-contact practice or training drills.
5. Players can return to competition with written permission from a licensed medical professional.

When an athlete suffers a hard hit, immediate help is required to assess if any physical injuries occurred. It is also essential to determine if the player may have received a concussion.

Returning to School

Sometimes returning to school can be difficult for young people recovering from a concussion. They can take various positive steps to cope with this process. First, they need to talk with their teachers, school counselors, and school nurses and explain their situation. The staff and each student can set up a plan on how to handle courses and schoolwork successfully. For example, young people might return to school part-time, reduce the number of courses, or transfer to less stressful subjects. Other possible adjustments include getting help with schoolwork or having more time to take tests and complete assignments. Some teens find that spending less time on the computer, reading, or writing is helpful. Brightly lit or loud rooms or hallways may interfere with their ability to pay attention or concentrate on classroom instructions. It's important to set up a quiet, supervised area at school where tired students may go to rest and then return to class when they feel better. They can increase their time in school as their brain injury heals.

A concussion can create challenges for students returning to school. It's important to ask for help if you need it.

GETTING SUPPORT WHILE HEALING

Recovery from a concussion can be complicated because the brain has been damaged. Although most athletes experience little or no physical evidence when a brain injury happens, changes in their thinking skills, memory, and personality may result. It may become difficult for these students to go to school or work, play sports, or have successful relationships.

Everyone reacts differently as they recover. They may feel sad, scared, angry, frustrated, tired, or anxious. It can be especially difficult if a concussion is keeping athletes away from their favorite activities. Some people become seriously depressed and feel deeply unhappy, worthless, hopeless, alone, or isolated.

Teens who have a concussion may need to ask for help with their daily routines. It can take courage to reach out to other people, but many resources are available. For example, sensitive, caring, supportive coaches and trainers can make the time away from the game far more healthy, productive, and healing. They can encourage teammates to also be supportive, encouraging, and accepting and continue to make the injured players feel like active and important members of the team. Young people can also talk with a parent, trusted adult or friend, teacher, school counselor, or health professional.

Entering into therapy can be very valuable when recovering from a concussion. Teens may want to see a therapist, which often requires a referral from their family doctor. Therapists are mental health professionals

The effects of a concussion may negatively affect daily life for teens. Therapy can help them learn different and healthier ways to manage emotions.

who design treatment plans for people based on the nature of their problems. The plan is made with the individual seeking help and may include therapy, medication, or a combination of the two.

Often known as talk therapy, psychotherapy is a process in which people talk one-on-one with a mental health professional about their feelings and problems and learn healthy ways to help themselves feel better. Psychotherapists help teens identify unique strong points within themselves that they can use to manage challenges and get through difficult times.

Group and family therapy can also be useful. Group therapy brings teens who are struggling with similar issues together to share experiences and provide support for each other. It allows them to practice new coping strategies and problem-solving skills with peers. When young people suddenly have a brain injury, family dynamics can sharply change in many ways and various challenges and problems arise. Concussed teens, for example, may need extra help, such as needing rides to school and doctor and therapy appointments. In family therapy, the entire family learns how to work together. Therapists help them develop communication skills, resolve issues, and promote strong bonds.

Taking Prescription Medications

Some people with a concussion become depressed, particularly if their recovery stretches beyond a few weeks. Agreeing to take an antidepressant is a strong step forward in dealing with their depression. Doctors frequently prescribe these medications to lift mood. They may also recommend antianxiety medicines or other drugs. A combination of psychotherapy and drug therapy often works best for depressed teens.

Using medications can take time and patience. Sometimes teens need to try several antidepressants before they find what works well. In addition, antidepressants need a few weeks or longer to begin affecting mood and can take six to eight weeks to be fully effective. Some of the possible side effects of antidepressants could seem worrisome, but they vary widely for

On June 9, 2015, nineteen-year-old Lacey shared her experiences about recovering from a concussion. The former high school player had four concussions in three months while playing basketball. Complications from the fourth concussion were serious. The once friendly teen became anxious and depressed and withdrew from friends. She also was highly sensitive to noise and light. Her mom was very caring and helpful during her daughter's healing process. A strong, positive relationship between Lacey and her mom developed. However, the teen's father and siblings were not supportive. They could not see anything physically wrong with her and thought she was pretending to have problems. Lacey graduated from high school and started college but continued taking prescription medications for postconcussion depression, anxiety, and sleep difficulties.

LACEY'S RECOVERY

everyone. Young people may experience no side effects, while others have minor discomfort. Side effects often lessen or disappear within a few weeks. The vast majority of these drugs are generally safe.

HELPING OTHERS

Sometimes friends, teammates, or parents of players who may have a concussion pick up on symptoms before trainers, coaches, parents, teachers, or other adults do. Red flags include headaches, vomiting, dizziness, confusion, fatigue, mood swings, neck pain, or pressure in the head.

Injured teens might have difficulty with balance, coordination, light, noise, or talking. These symptoms can be serious. It's important to immediately contact a coach, trainer, or responsible adult. In emergency situations, call 911 or a local hospital emergency room right away.

Teens should be patient, supportive, and encouraging of their friends or family members who have a concussion. They may need to remind themselves that changes in emotions and functioning are the result of a brain injury. Recovery can take time.

People may not recognize the symptoms of a concussion right away. A friend or family member might be the first person to notice the effects of a concussion later on.

CHAPTER 6

TODAY AND THE FUTURE

Many people are working to tackle the growing concerns about concussions. As scientists learn more about brain injuries and their causes, sports regulations will continue evolving to increase the safety of players. Better screening methods for concussions and protective equipment for sports and recreational activities are being developed. These steps and increasing awareness about concussions will help everyone stay safer in their daily life. The best treatment for a concussion is prevention.

CONCUSSION LAWS PROTECTING YOUTH ATHLETES

All fifty states and the District of Columbia have laws on the management of concussions in school athletics. The laws are also known as return-to-play guidelines. The rules vary from state to state, but the regulations have three common parts. First, any players with signs or symptoms of a concussion must be immediately removed from the game. Next, they are not allowed to return to play on the day of the injury. Finally, all athletes need to be evaluated and cleared by a licensed medical professional before they can return to play. Many states also require coaches to complete a concussion education program, such as the one offered through the National Federation of State High School Associations, and provide parents with concussion information materials.

In 2015, the Florida High School Athletic Association became the first organization in the United States to

Former pro football players represented by attorneys are going to court for physical damages. The lawsuits claim that players' brains have been repeatedly injured because of hard blows to the head without adequate safety equipment.

require high school athletes in all sports to complete a course on concussions before competition begins. A year later, a bill called the Youth Sports Concussion Act was introduced into Congress. Passage of the law would allow federal safety standards to be established for protective sports equipment, such as helmets, custom mouth guards, sensors, and headbands. Many manufacturers claim their products prevent head injuries, but no research has conclusively shown that any of these items decrease the risk of concussions.

The Centers for Disease Control (CDC) has asked Congress for funds to create and manage a National Concussion Surveillance System to track and monitor information about concussions every year. The data would help the agency better understand this public health problem and learn the best ways to protect children, teens, and adults.

Better Sports Gear, Testing, and Diagnosing

Today's sporting equipment cannot prevent concussions or entirely eliminate their risk in any sport. Scientists are trying to change that. Some football helmets have been, and are being, developed that can give doctors, trainers, and coaches information about what is happening to the brains of athletes as they play. These helmets use accelerometers, or impact sensors, that measure in real time the force and number of impacts players receive. Trainers, coaches, and team doctors can monitor this information on computers from the sidelines. If a hit registers a high level of force, the player is removed from the game and watched for symptoms of a concussion. Data provided by accelerators may help manufacturers create equipment that would lower the risk of concussions. Currently, some companies are increasing the padding in helmets where most impacts occur. Other businesses are developing football helmets made with new flexible materials to better absorb the impact energy from head blows. Another area of research focuses on improving the fit of helmets, which might provide added protection against head injuries.

Equipment changes that could make other sports safer include softer baseballs and soccer balls. These balls have soft, spongy cores. Some scientists think that if these balls are routinely used, fewer head injuries would occur. A number of baseball helmets are now equipped with face masks. Using the masks consistently may lower the number of head injuries in baseball players.

Most concussions in soccer occur when athletes run into each other, but some happen when players head a ball. Girls who play youth soccer have higher concussion rates than boys who play soccer and are the same age. The statistic may be because the size and weight of the balls are not matched to the age and gender of the players. The neck and shoulder muscles of girls are not as large and strong as those of boys. Some manufacturers are designing smaller and lighter soccer balls that might be safer for female players.

During the 2014 White House Science Fair, President Barack Obama looked at the concussion cushion football helmet project from Maria Hanes, of Santa Cruz, California.

NEW TESTING AND DIAGNOSING METHODS

Research is ongoing to identify reliable and convenient methods to detect concussions. Scientists are developing a quick blood test to identify concussions in injured players on the sidelines. These small devices would analyze a few drops of blood for a protein linked with concussions. New equipment that measures changes in eye movement associated with head injuries might also provide doctors with a rapid, objective method for detecting concussions. Trainers and coaches would be able to use the blood or eye movement tests on the sidelines. Other researchers are working on new brain imaging techniques that would show concussion damage.

In 2012, the NFL and National Health Institutes formed a partnership to create the Health Sports and Health Research Program. The NFL donated $30 million to help conduct medical research on brain injuries, including concussions. Research funded through the Sports and Health Research Program is implemented and managed by the National Institutes of Health. However, the partnership could mean that the NFL has some involvement with potential research studies, which may lead to moral and ethical conflicts and compromises.

Some large corporations and sports organizations are jointly funding brain research. Recently, Jeff Immelt, CEO of General Electric, and the National Football League announced a research program to improve the safety of pro football players.

Wearing a helmet is an important safety action everyone can take to protect their head when enjoying a recreational activity, such as bicycling. During a fall or collision, much of the impact energy is absorbed by the headgear, rather than the head and brain. Bicycle helmets are required by law for youth under the age of sixteen in twenty-two states and the District of Columbia. All helmets made or sold in the United States must meet the standards of the Consumer Product Safety Commission (CPSC). (The CPSC's standards can be read online at http://ww.cpsc.gov.) Before bicycling, teens should check that their helmet is level on their head and the strap is snugly and securely fastened.

People can wear bicycle helmets for other recreational activities too, including in-line skating, roller skating, or riding a scooter. However, other activities require special helmets specifically designed for them, such as skiing or snowboarding.

WEARING HELMETS DURING RECREATIONAL ACTIVITIES

RAISING PUBLIC AWARENESS OF CONCUSSIONS

Despite the increased coverage of concussions in the news, the majority of people in the United States do not understand these traumatic brain injuries. The Brain Injury Association of America reported that in a recent Harris Poll, nearly 90 percent of those surveyed did not know what a concussion is, and almost 70 percent did not know that a person can have a concussion without getting a blow to the head. Less than half of the study participants knew all of the common signs and symptoms of a possible concussion.

The good news is that more information about these brain injuries continues to reach the public. On December 25, 2015, Sony Pictures released the movie *Concussion*. Actor Will Smith played Dr. Bennett Omalu, the doctor who found that repeated concussions in professional football can result in chronic traumatic encephalopathy. In January 2016, the CDC published a guide for the media to better

Actor Will Smith and Bennet Omalu appeared together to promote their movie, *Concussion*, which helped raise awareness of brain injuries.

SAVING COLE

During high school, Cole sustained a concussion while wrestling. The emergency department doctor recommended that he rest for a month before returning to play his favorite sport. Instead, the teen stayed away for one week and then, without telling anyone, snuck off to practice. Unfortunately, after finishing a drill, a teammate accidently rolled onto Cole's head. Cole was slow to stand up, appeared dazed, and could not answer simple questions. He also had a severe headache. The coach had taken the CDC's HEADS UP concussion training and quickly determined that the teen needed immediate medical care. The teen's symptoms lingered for months, and he was advised never to wrestle again. Cole credits his coach for saving his life.

inform the public about concussions and other traumatic brain injuries.

This health agency also is leading a national campaign called "HEADS UP: Concussion in Youth Sports" to help raise awareness of concussions. The CDC developed the free tool kit for parents, coaches, sports officials, and students involved in sports. The program contains posters, videos, and other educational materials on how to prevent, recognize, and respond to a concussion. In addition, anyone can take a short, online course that provides information on keeping athletes safe from concussions. The free course and kits are available on the CDC website (http://www.cdc.gov/headsup/youthsports).

The CDC also offers an app called "HEADS UP Concussion and Helmet Safety." It explains how to spot a possible concussion or other serious brain injuries and what to do. The app also presents information on correct helmet fit, safety, and maintenance. This free resource can be found on the agency's website (http://www.cdc.gov/headsup/resources/app.html).

Positive Prevention Strategies

Young people get most of their concussions in motor vehicle and bicycle accidents or while playing sports. By wearing a seatbelt, they can lower the risk of head injuries in a car crash. A good habit is to put the seatbelt on before the vehicle is started. Teens can also put their safety first by turning down invitations to ride with friends if the car does not have enough seatbelts for everyone. The chances of a crash while driving significantly increase when drivers text or dial on a mobile phone, speed, or are under the influence of alcohol or drugs. Routine maintenance of motorized vehicles can help prevent collisions.

Sports are regulated to provide maximum fun for participants and enjoyment for the audience. Many rules are in place to keep players safe. The National Federation of State High School Associations establishes the rules of competition for most high school sports. Guidelines include that coaches teach their athletes the safest techniques to tackle in football and head the ball during soccer competition.

For teens, enjoying regular exercise, eating nutritious foods, and getting enough sleep every night are positive behaviors that foster strong physical and mental growth.

Players must also take responsibility for their safety. Consistently wearing the appropriate protective equipment for their sport is important, which may include helmets, shin guards, padding, or eye and mouth guards. These items need to fit properly and should be regularly maintained. Everyone—players, coaches, trainers, parents, and other school officials—needs to keep in mind that anyone who may have a concussion needs to be pulled from the game and tested. Pressuring injured athletes to play increases the risk of second impact syndrome. The CDC's fact sheets and other materials emphasize, "It's better to miss one game than the whole season."

Following a healthy lifestyle helps athletes perform well in school and sports and at work. When young people feel rested, alert, and capable of handling daily challenges, they tend to have fewer falls and other accidents. Some simple steps they can take are getting enough sleep and eating healthy meals and snacks that include vegetables, fruits, and whole grains. Whether it's to unwind, socialize, or keep fit, exercising regularly is vital to the health and well-being of teens. Exercise keeps you strong and improves balance and coordination. There are sports for everyone, including playing team sports or participating in recreational activities, such as hiking, swimming, biking, dancing, jogging, skating, skiing, or marital arts. Being around positive and supportive people is enjoyable and keeps spirits high.

Teens can help educate other people about learning how to protect themselves from a concussion. For example, they might team up with friends and sponsor a concussion information booth at a school or sporting event. Student councils could sponsor an essay contest with the topic "Protect Your Brain from Concussions." Local medical professionals or an association could judge the winning essay and provide a scholarship to the winner.

Concussions are a serious medical condition. Unfortunately, head injuries can never be completely avoided, but everyone can take steps to decrease the likelihood of a concussion. Education and improved protective equipment will be effective in reducing concussions when people use that knowledge and take steps to protect themselves. The future is bright that the frequency and severity of concussions can be reduced.

GLOSSARY

accelerometer An impact sensor that measures how strong a force is to the head and body during a collision and can immediately relay the information to sports staff.

amnesia A loss of memory.

athletic trainer A health care professional who specializes in the prevention, diagnosis, and treatment of injuries.

baseline A test place from which to start; a test with which to compare another test.

chronic traumatic encephalopathy (CTE) A progressive, degenerative disease of the brain found in people with a history of repeated concussions.

cognitive Involving cognition, which is the process of knowing and becoming aware—thinking, learning, and judging.

computed tomography (CT) A computerized method of taking special pictures of the brain.

concussion An injury to the brain that is caused by something hitting the head or body very hard.

consciousness Mentally awake and alert.

degenerative Causing the body to become weaker and less able to function as time passes.

dementia A usually progressive condition marked by decreased cognitive functioning.

depression A mental illness in which sadness overwhelms one's life.

diagnosis The identification of a disease following an examination.

magnetic resonance imaging (MRI) A method that uses powerful magnets and radio waves to help create a picture of the inside of a person.

neurologist A physician specializing in the diagnosis and treatment of diseases of the nervous system

neuron A nerve cell.

neuropsychological test An assessment tool that evaluates brain function, including information processing, memory, attention, learning, and language.

orientation Knowledge of who you are, where you are, and what time it is.

postconcussion syndrome (PCS) A disorder in which a combination of symptoms, such as headaches and dizziness, lasts for weeks or months after a concussion.

progressive Tending to become more severe over time.

second impact syndrome (SIS) A rare but serious condition caused by sustaining a second concussion before an earlier concussion has healed.

tau A protein in the brain.

therapist A person trained to help people recover from a mental or physical illness or cope with daily life.

therapy Treatment for a mental condition or a physical disease.

traumatic brain injury A blow, bump, or jolt to the head that disrupts the normal functions of the brain.

FOR MORE INFORMATION

American Brain Coalition
6257 Quantico Lane N.
Maple Grove, MN 55331
(763) 557-2913
Website: http://www.americanbraincoalition.org

The American Brain Coalition is a nonprofit organization that seeks to advance the understanding of the functions of the brain and to reduce the burden of brain disorders through public advocacy.

Brain Injury Association of America
1608 Spring Hill Road, Suite 110
Vienna, VA 22182
(800) 444-6443
Website: http://www.biausa.org

The Brain Injury Association of America strives to advance brain injury prevention, research, treatment, and education and provides support to people living with traumatic brain injury and their families.

Brain Injury Association of Canada
440 Laurier Avenue West
Ottawa, ON K1R 7X6
Canada
(866) 977-2492
Website: http://braininjurycanada.ca

The Brain Injury Association of Canada is a national organization that works to improve life for Canadians affected by brain injury. The organization also promotes prevention, research, and education in partnership with other associations.

Brain Trauma Foundation

1 Broadway, 6th Floor
New York City, NY 10004
(212) 722-0608
Website: https://www.braintrauma.org

The Brain Trauma Foundation develops best practice guidelines for medical professionals to improve the outcome of people with traumatic brain injury.

Centers for Disease Control and Prevention

1600 Clifton Road
Atlanta, GA 30333
(800) 232-4636
Website: http://www.cdc.gov

This federal agency provides information about health-related topics. Its HEADS UP program educates athletes, parents, coaches, and sports officials about concussions.

National Athletic Trainers Association

1620 Valwood Parkway, Suite 115
Carrollton, TX 75006
(214) 637-6282
Website: https://www.nata.org

The Athletic Trainers Association offers information on athletic training, youth sports safety, and brain injuries.

National Federation of State High School Associations

690 W. Washington Street
Indianapolis, IN 46204
(317) 972-6900
Website: https://www.nfhs.org

The National Federation of State High School Associations establishes consistent standards and rules for competition at the high school level.

National Institute of Neurological Disorders and Stroke

NIH Neurological Institute
PO Box 5801
Bethesda, MD 20824
(800) 352-9424
Website: http://www.ninds.nih.gov

This federal agency conducts and funds research on brain and nervous system disorders.

National Youth Sports Safety Foundation

60 Thoreau Street, Suite 288
Concord, Massachusetts 01742
(800) 474-5201
Website: http://www.momsteam.com

The National Youth Sports Safety Foundation provides educational information on the prevention of youth sports injuries.

Parachute

150 Eglinton Avenue East, Suite 300
Toronto, ON M4P 1E8
Canada
Tel: 647-776-5100
(888) 537-7777
Website: http://www.parachutecanada.org

Parachute is a national charitable organization dedicated to preventing injuries, including concussions, through education.

WEBSITES

Because of the changing nature of Internet links, Rosen Publishing has developed an online list of websites related to the subject of this book. This site is updated regularly. Please use this link to access this list:

http://www.rosenlinks.com/411/conc

FOR FURTHER READING

Almond, Steve. *Against Football: One Fan's Reluctant Manifesto*. Brooklyn, NY: Melville House, 2015.

Asselin, Kristine Carlson. *What You Need to Know About Concussions*. North Mankato, MN: Capstone Press, 2015.

Butler, Colleen. *Concussion Recovery: Rebuilding the Injured Brain*. Seattle, WA: CreateSpace Independent Publishing Platform, 2012.

Engelland, Ann. *It's All in Your Head: Everyone's Guide to Managing Concussions*. West Harrison, NY: Ann L Engelland, MD PLLC, 2012.

Esherick, Joan. *Brain Injury (Living with a Special Need)*. Broomall, PA: Mason Crest Publishers, 2014.

Fay, Gail. *Sports: The Ultimate Teen Guide*. Lanham, MD: Scarecrow Press, 2012.

Goldsmith, Connie. *Traumatic Brain Injury: From Concussion to Coma*. Minneapolis, MN: Twenty-First Century Books, 2014.

Hudson, Maryann. *High-Pressure Youth Sports*. Minneapolis, MN: Abdo Publishing, 2014.

Irwin, Sue. *Safety Stars: Players Who Fought to Make the Hard-hitting Game of Professional Hockey Safer*. Toronto, ON, Canada: Lorimer Recordbooks, 2015.

Kamberg, Mary-Lane. *Sports Concussions*. New York, NY: Rosen Publishing, 2011.

Laskas, Jeanne Marie. *Concussion*. New York, NY: Random House Trade Paperbacks, 2015.

McClafferty, Carla Killough. *Fourth Down and Inches: Concussions and Football's Make-or-Break Moment.* Minneapolis, MN: Lerner Publishing, 2013.

Riley, Joelle. *Your Nervous System.* Minneapolis, MN: Lerner Classroom, 2012.

Robinson, Antwala. *YOU Rule! Take Charge of Your Health and Life: A Healthy Lifestyle Guide for Teens.* Atlanta, GA: Wellness Agent, 2014.

Schwartz, Tina P. *Depression: The Ultimate Teen Guide.* Lanham, Maryland: Rowman & Littlefield Publishers, 2014.

Song, Suk-young. *The Nervous System.* St. Louis, MO: Turtleback, 2013.

Sports in America. Ipswich, MA: Greyhouse Publishing, 2013.

Watson, Stephanie. *Brain Injuries in Football.* Minneapolis, MN: Abdo Publishing, 2014.

White, William, Ashare Alan, and Katharine White. *Winning The War Against Concussions In Youth Sports: Brain and Life Saving Solutions For Preventing and Healing Youth Sports Head Injuries.* Seattle, WA: CreateSpace Independent Publishing Platform, 2014.

Wilcox, Christine. *Is Enough Being Done to Protect Athletes from Concussions?* San Diego: Referencepoint Press, 2015.

BIBLIOGRAPHY

American Association of Neurological Surgeons. "Concussion," Retrieved February 16, 2016. http://www.aans.org/patient%20information/conditions%20and%20treatments/concussion.

Bakhos, Lisa L., Gregory R. Lockhart, Richard Myers, and James G. Linakis. "Emergency Department Visits for Concussion in Young Child Athletes." *Pediatrics*. Retrieved February 16, 2016. http://pediatrics.aappublications.org/content/126/3/e550.

Borzi, Pat. "Amanda Kessel, Top College Player Out of Action Since Sochi, Returns." *New York Times*, February 6, 2016. http://www.nytimes.com/2016/02/07/sports/hockey/amanda-kessel-top-college-player-out-of-action-since-sochi-returns.html?_r=2.

Brain Injury Alliance of New Jersey. "Concussion Management." Retrieved February 16, 2016. http://sportsconcussion.bianj.org/concussion-management/.

Brain Injury Association of America. "How is Will Smith Helping to Raise Awareness about Concussions?" December 31, 2015. http://www.biausa.org/announcements/how-is-will-smith-helping-to-raise-awareness-about-concussions.

Cantu, Robert, and Mark Hyman. *Concussions and Our Kids: America's Leading Expert on How to Protect Young Athletes and Keep Sports Safe.* Boston, MA: Houghton Mifflin Harcourt, 2012.

Carroll, Linda. *The Concussion Crisis: Anatomy of a Silent Epidemic.* New York City, NY: Simon & Schuster, 2013.

Esty, Mary Lee, and C. M. Shifflett. *Conquering Concussion.* Sewickley, PA: Round Earth Publishing, 2014.

Lacey. "Former Basketball Player, Lacey, Shares Her Concussion Story." June 9, 2015. https://www.triaxtec.com/stories/lacey-shares-her-concussion-story.

Lemke, Christopher (coach for Two Harbors High School, Lake Superior School District, Minnesota), in discussion with the author, March 2016.

Martin, Jill. "NFL Acknowledges CTE Link with Football. Now what?" March 16, 2016. http://www.cnn.com/2016/03/15/health/nfl-cte-link.

Meehan, William Paul. *Kids, Sports, and Concussion: A Guide for Coaches and Parents.* Santa Barbara, CA: Praeger, 2011.

Moser, Rosemarie Scolaro. *Ahead of the Game: The Parent's Guide to Youth Sports Concussion.* Hanover, NH: Dartmouth College Press, 2012.

National Institute of Neurological Disorders and Stroke. "NINDS Traumatic Brain Injury Information Page." February 11, 2016. http:/www.ninds.nih.gov/disorders/tbi/detail_tbi.htm.

Olson, Jeremy. "Minnesota Hospitals Launch 'Nation's Largest' Concussion Study." *Star Tribune*, March 9, 2016. http://www.startribune.com/minnesota-hospitals-launch-nation-s-largest-concussion-study/371531011.

Stoler, Diane Roberts, and Barbara Albers Hill. *Coping with Concussion and Mild Traumatic Brian Injury: A Guide to Living with the Challenges Associated with Post-Concussion Syndrome and Brain Trauma.* New York City, NY: Avery, 2013.

U.S. Centers for Disease Control and Prevention. "Cole's Story: Coach Saves a Wrestler's Life by Knowing Concussion Signs and Symptoms." February 16, 2016. http://www.cdc.gov/headsup/pdfs/stories/coles_story_one_pager-a.pdf.

U.S. Centers for Disease Control and Prevention. "HEADS UP." January 4, 2016. http://www.cdc.gov /HEADSUP.

U.S. Centers for Disease Control and Prevention. "Traumatic Brain Injury: Get the Facts." January 22, 2016. http:// www.cdc.gov/traumaticbraininjury/get_the_facts.html.

Waldron, Travis. "Senators Push For More Equipment Oversight To Combat Youth Sports Concussions." Huffington Post, February 5, 2016. http://www. huffingtonpost.com/entry/youth-football-concussions -tom-udall_us_56b4a9d4e4b01d80b245ddd

INDEX

ABOUT THE AUTHOR

Judy Monroe Peterson has earned two master's degrees and is the author of more than seventy educational books for young people, including books on many health and life skills topics. She is a former health care, technical, and academic librarian and college faculty member, biologist, and research scientist. She has taught courses at 3M, the University of Minnesota, and Lake Superior College.

PHOTO CREDITS

Cover, pp. 1, 18–19 Photographee.eu /Shutterstock.com; p. 5 Thomas Barrat/Shutterstock.com; p. 9 Fcscafeine/Shutterstock .com; pp. 12–13 Sergey Nivens/Shutterstock.com; pp. 14–15 bikeriderlondon/Shutterstock.com; p. 21 IvanRiver/ Shutterstock.com; p. 25 think4photop/Shutterstock.com; pp. 28–29 FamVeld/Shutterstock.com; pp. 30–31 Donald Linscott/Shutterstock.com; pp. 36–37 Dmitry Kalinovsky/ Shutterstock.com; p. 39 Mat Hayward/Shutterstock.com; p. 40–41 CruZeWizard/Shutterstock.com; pp. 44–45 Miami Herald/Tribune News Service/Getty Images; pp. 48–49 anekoho/Shutterstock.com; pp. 50–51, 69 Syda Productions/ Shutterstock.com; pp. 54–55, 74 Monkey Business Images/ Shutterstock.com; p. 57 michaeljung/Shutterstock.com; p. 59 Jochen Schoenfeld/Shutterstock.com; pp. 64–65 Pete Marovich/ Getty Images; p. 72 Aspen Photo/Shutterstock.com; pp. 76–77 wavebreakmedia/Shutterstock.com; pp. 80–81 Antonio Guillem/ Shutterstock.com; p. 83 Chicago Tribune/Tribune News Service/Getty Images; pp. 86–87 White House Pool/Corbis News/Getty Images; p. 88 Allison Joyce/Getty Images; pp. 90–91 Jerod Harris/Getty Images; pp. 94–95 The Washington Post/Getty Images.

Designer: Les Kanturek
Editor and Photo Researcher: Bethany Bryan